Copyright ©2018 AMB University, AmbKids Academy Publishing Division

ISBN-13: 978-1727700015
ISBN-: 1727700015

All rights reserved. Printed in the United States of America. No Part of this book may be used or reproduced in any manner whatsoever without written permission.

Order Copies ambkidsacademy@gmail.com

Via Author-Director, or Order Form in the back of this book. Order Forms include reads, and learning tool books published by ambKids academy.

Youth, Parents, Teachers, Professionals interested in Publishing under the amb university publishing forum please email ambkidsacademy@gmail.com or ambassociatedpress@gmail.com Please place inquiry in the subject line.

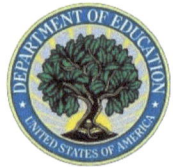 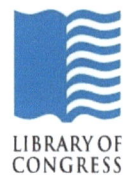 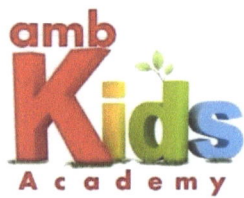

Greetings, Parents, Teachers, and Youth,

We wish to welcome you to ambKids Academy. ambKids Academy is an advocacy project with a goal of improving state wide test scores, reading, writing, and life skills training, through learning tool workbooks, publishing books with target messages for youth in areas that will build self-esteem, healthy body image, and social-economic enrichment to better serve the youth in our communities. We have a publishing platform for students, teachers, parents, and professionals interested in writing programs, educational reads, manuals-textbooks.

At ambKids Academy we, provide youth with the tools and teaching for entrepreneurship, through training and mentorship. Our mission is to cultivate our cities and towns by coupling enrichment and educational programs to improve the overall sustainability of mental health thus improving morality, grades, and test scores.

Our Project Goal:

- Is to improve reading and writing fundamentals for grades K-12, by providing age appropriate learning tools, launching AMB Junior writer's academy, and providing the necessary training needed to appropriately market and brand ideas founded by our authors, parents, professionals.

- Provide a Publishing platform for young writers age 5-18, parent-child projects, that focus on life skills, reading, writing, math, and entrepreneurial development.

- Provide a publishing Platform for Professionals interested in writing text books, self-help, workbooks and memoirs.

- Provide enrichment programs for youth which focus on anti-violence in schools, healthy eating, mental health-self-esteem building, and trade school training.

- Provide study skill notebooks directly related to the standardized LEAP test.

Our Objective:

- Service the Youth Market
- Publish low-cost products and distribute to schools and districts, to consumers, reading clubs, book fairs and through retail stores and online stores.

Provide Quality Service: We INTEND to provide our customers with courteous, prompt, and dependable service. We intend to present a company that has a reputation for timely deliveries of educational supplies and learning tools. The AMB Project has three segments:

AmbKids Academy-publishes young authors age 5-17 as well as parent-child projects. This project developed to encourage school age children to write and use their imagination to create narrative stories, thus increasing cognitive development, social skills, writing and reading improvement, and test scores.

ambKids Academy also provides learning tool workbooks for students K-12, which distribute to schools, consumers, and professionals. Learning Tool Workbooks focus on school curriculum for age appropriate studies, such as, numbers, alphabet, sight words, math, science, and geography.

-

Amb Junior writers of America-Publishing house is for authors age 18-21 was developed to teach youth the business of publishing books, writing, marketing, and branding products.

Amb Associated Press, is a coalition of Professionals, Parents, and Teachers with the common goal of improving education with target areas in reading, writing, math, and science, and providing Professional manuals in trade areas of expertise.

Origin of the Amb Project:

ambKids Academy and Amb Associated Press, is a Publishing Imprint of AMB University a distance education College for the Creative Arts. AMB University offers Educational Programs in the areas of Product Development, Brand Marketing, Grant Writing and Research.

The AMB University Publishing arena, ambKids academy and Amb Associated Press would like to invite your school, teachers, parents and students, to join and support our advocacy to improve study skills, reading, writing, and math. We would like to provide enrichment programs and learning tools for young writers to publish books and learn how to build a business behind their products.

A quarterly catalog of our works will be distributed to parents, staff, and teachers. We would like to provide your schools library with a selection of learning tools and include these reads and workbooks in school fairs and publications.

We thank you, ambassadors of education for your support in improving cognitive development and life skill training in students of our surrounding communities.

Warm regards,

President-Founder-Project Developer,
Professor, Aija M. Butler
Professor Aija M. Butler

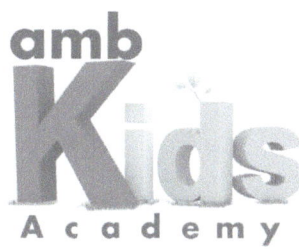

Give me an "A" Academic Society

Presents

"Halloween"
Coloring Fun

Sponsored By:
ambKids Academy

This Book Belongs To:

_____

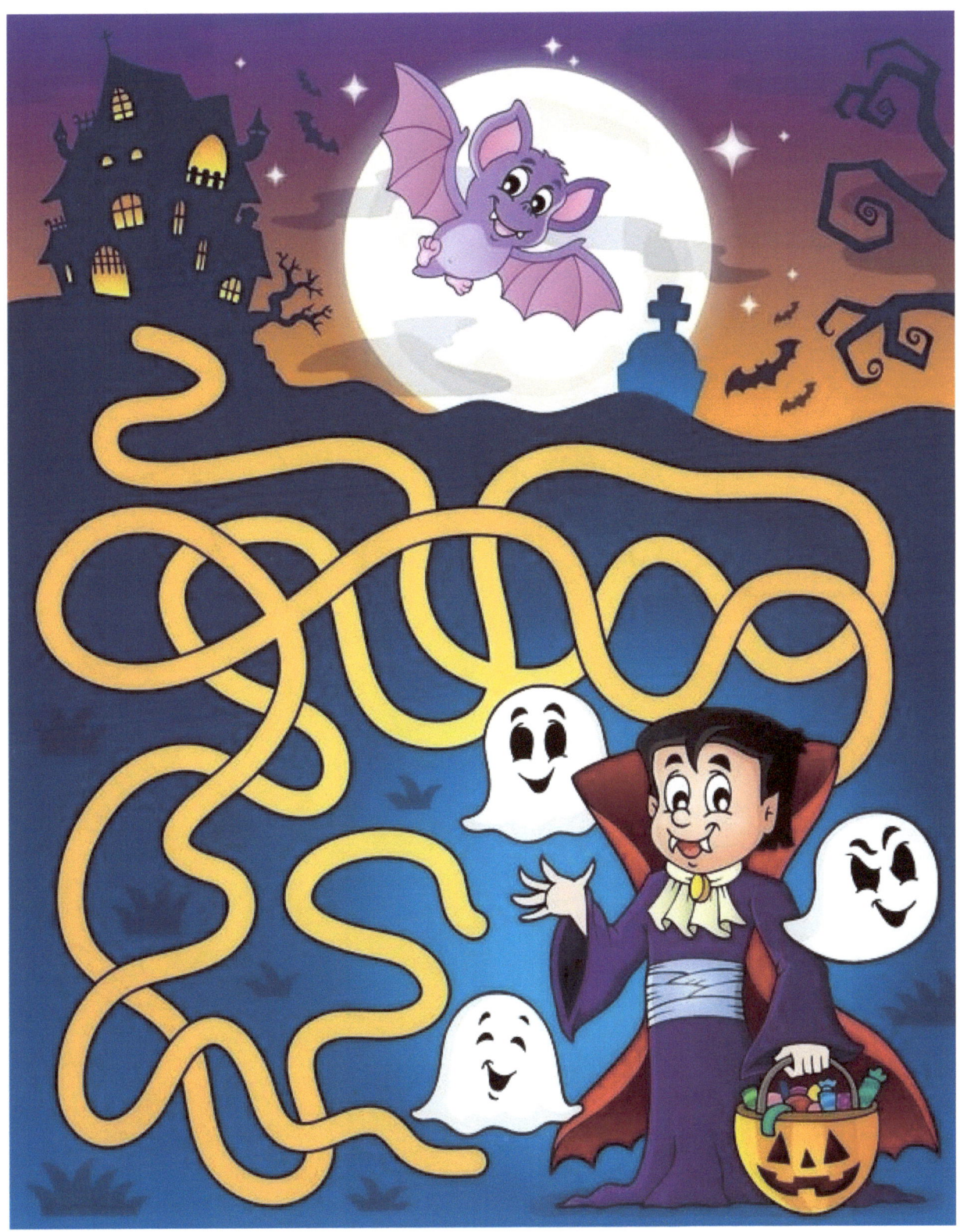

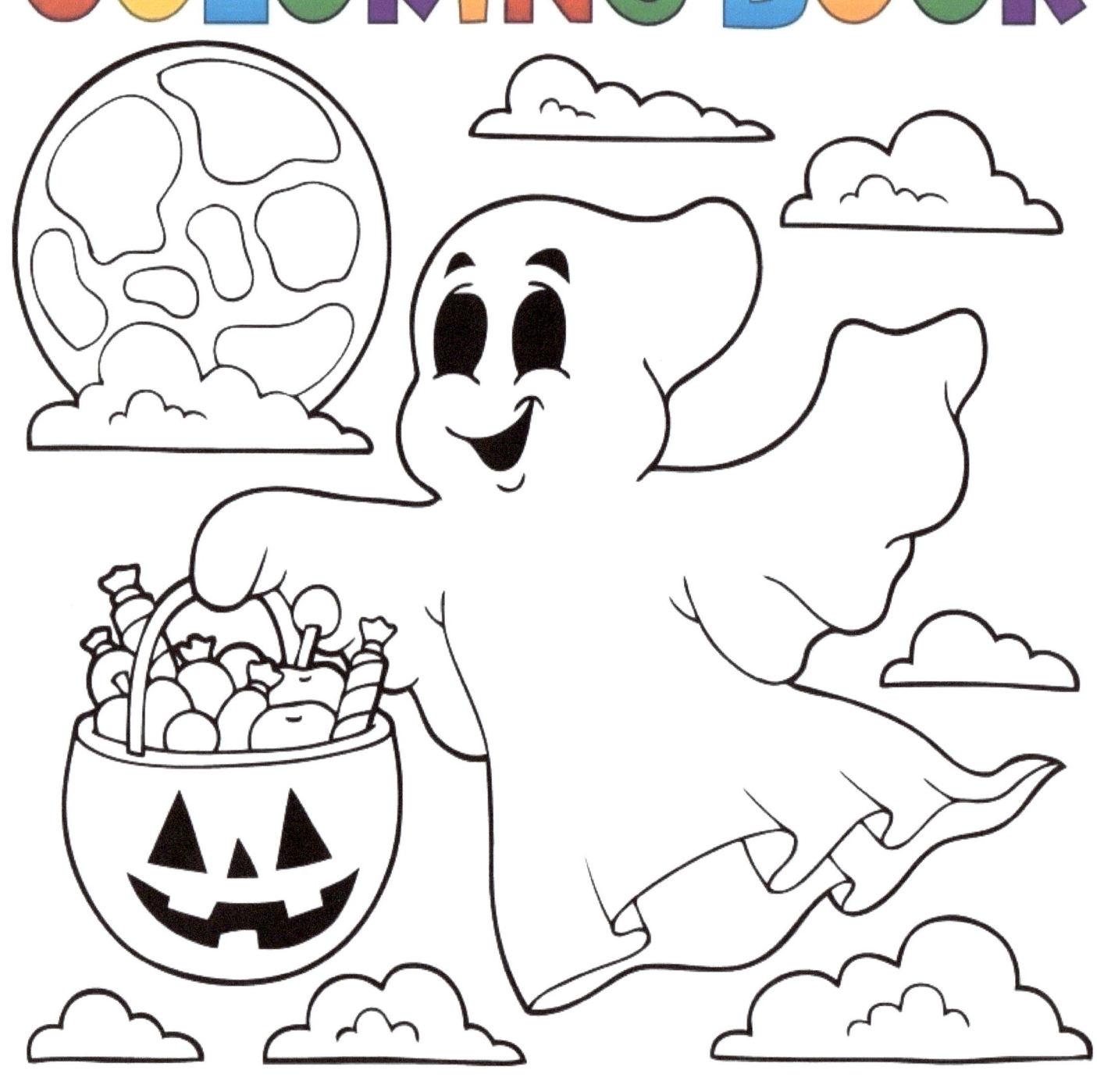

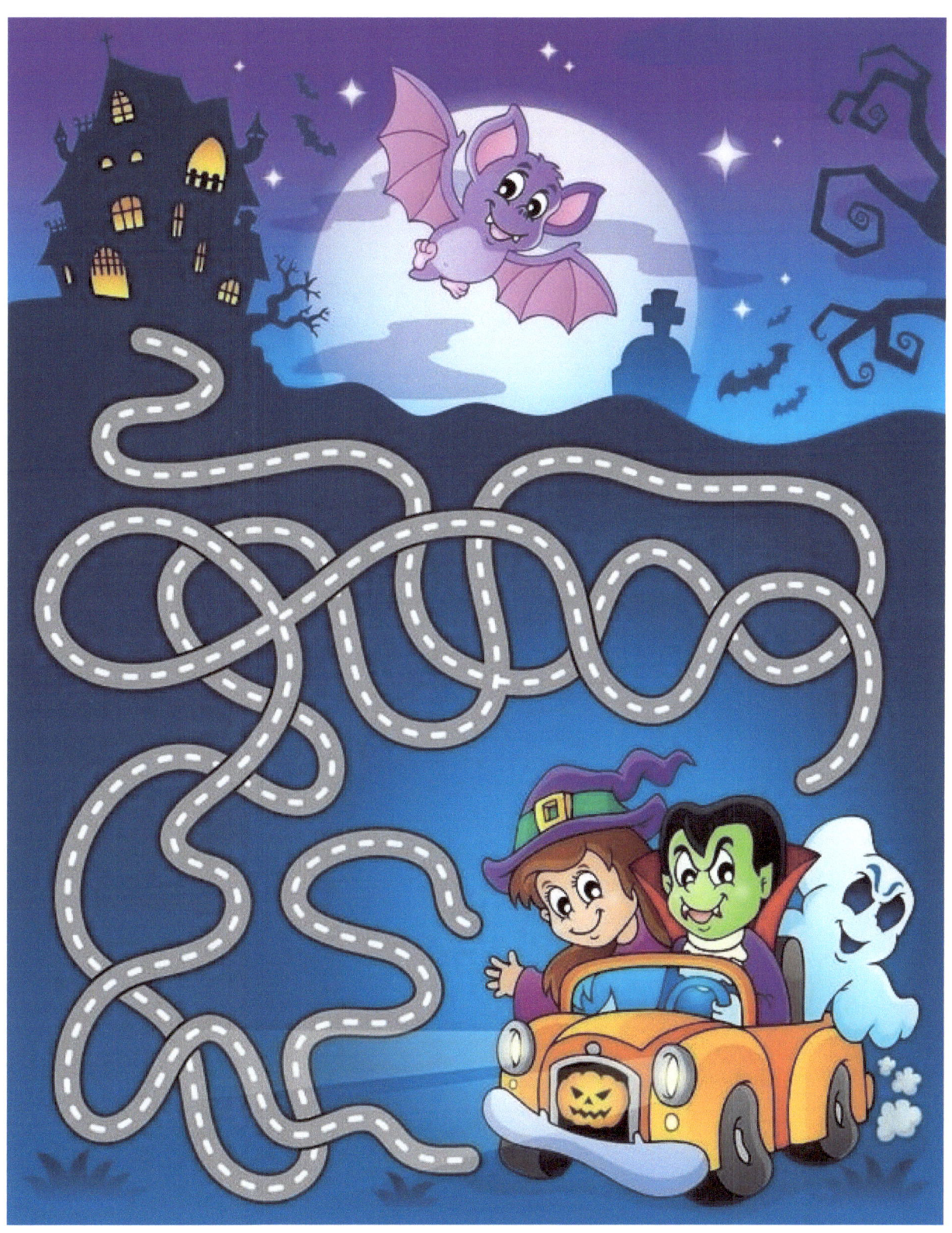

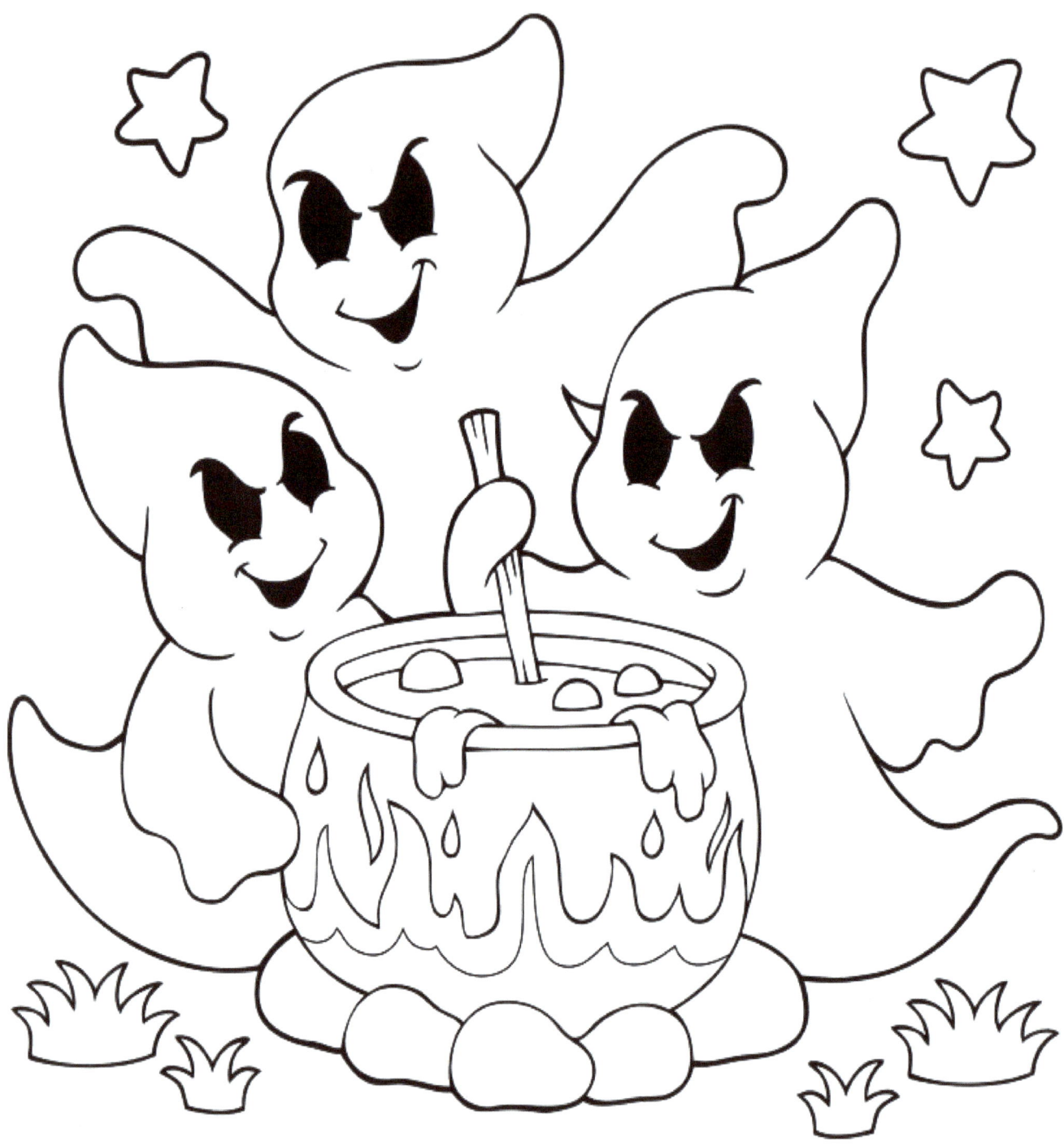

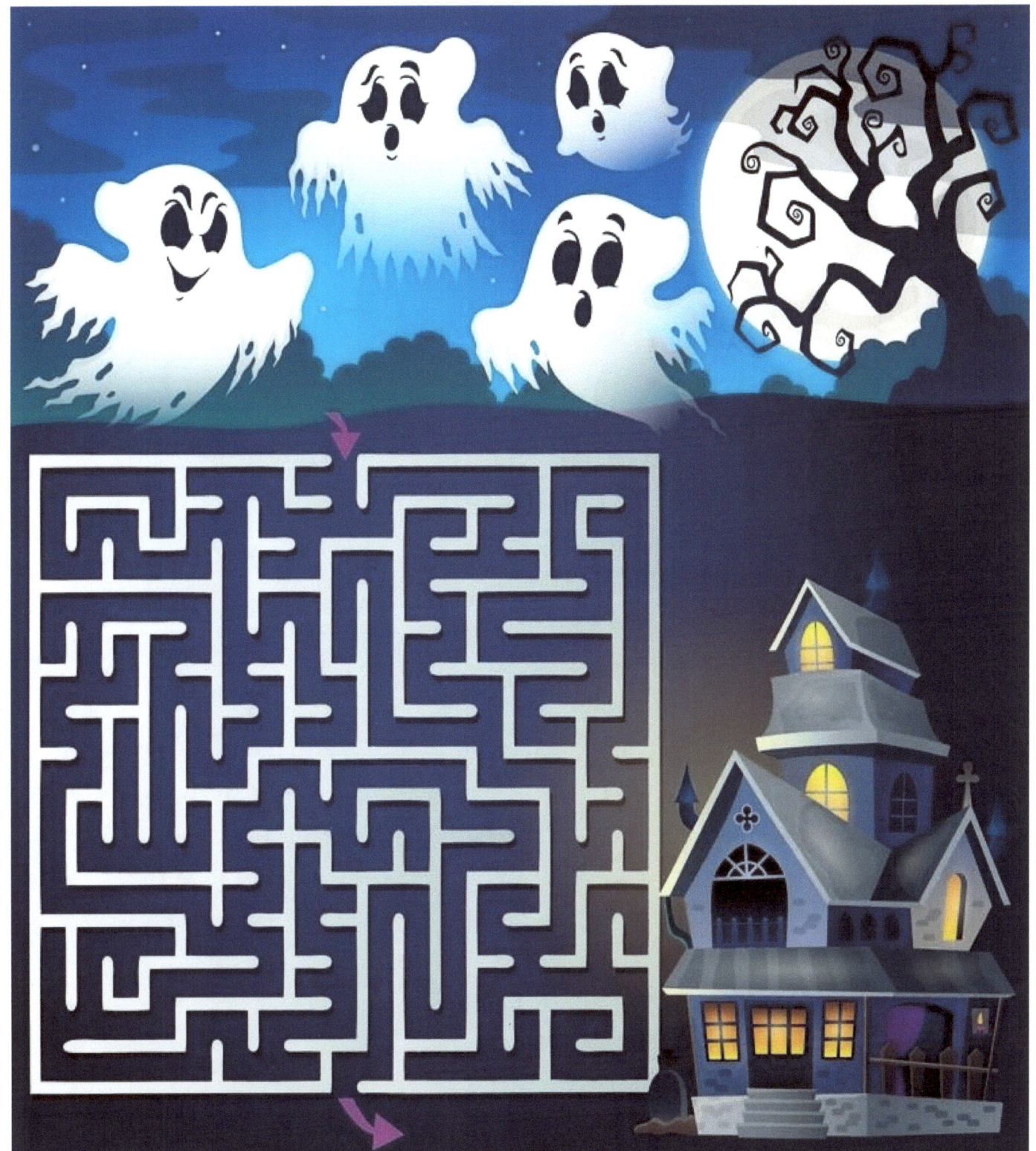

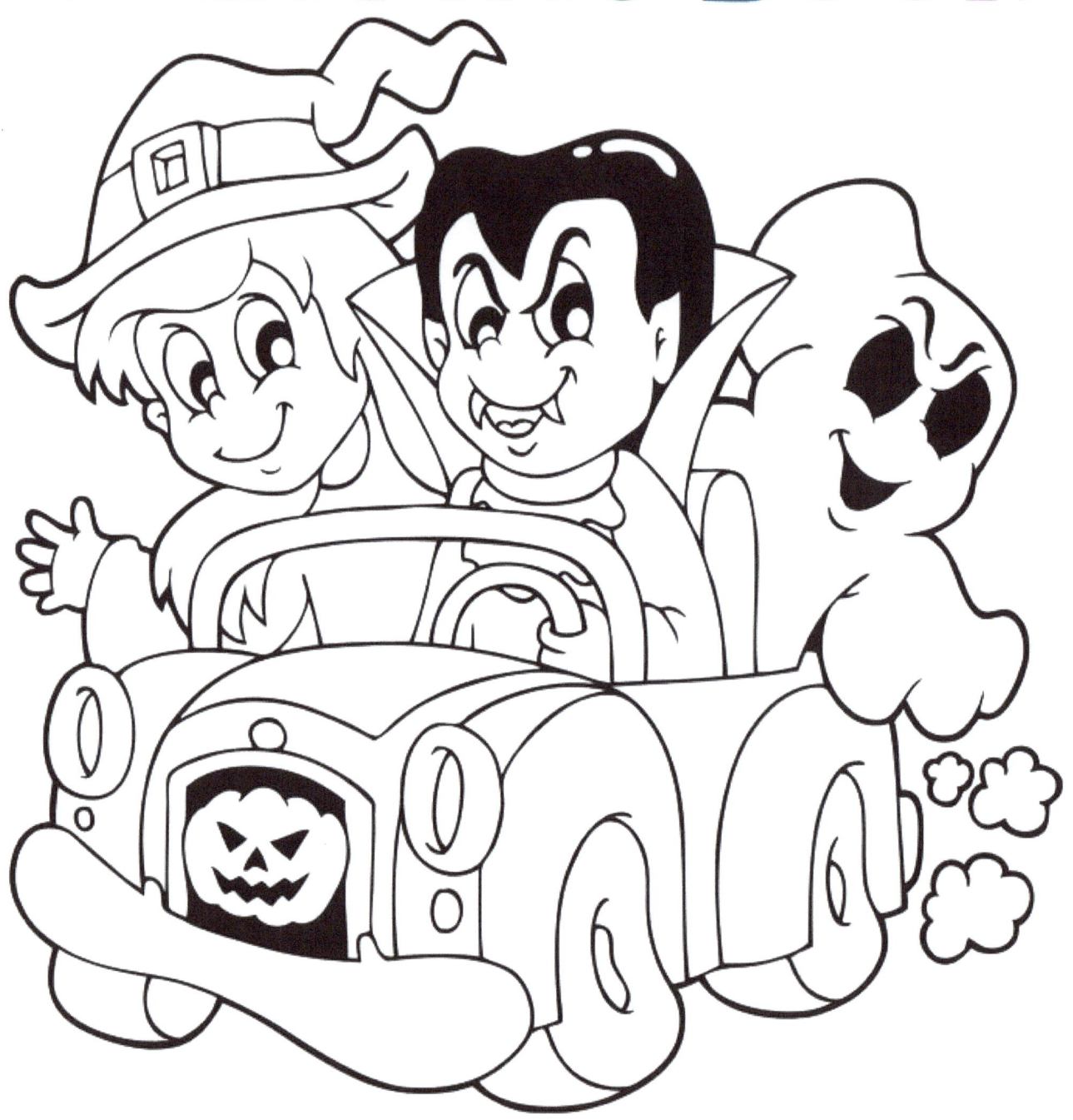

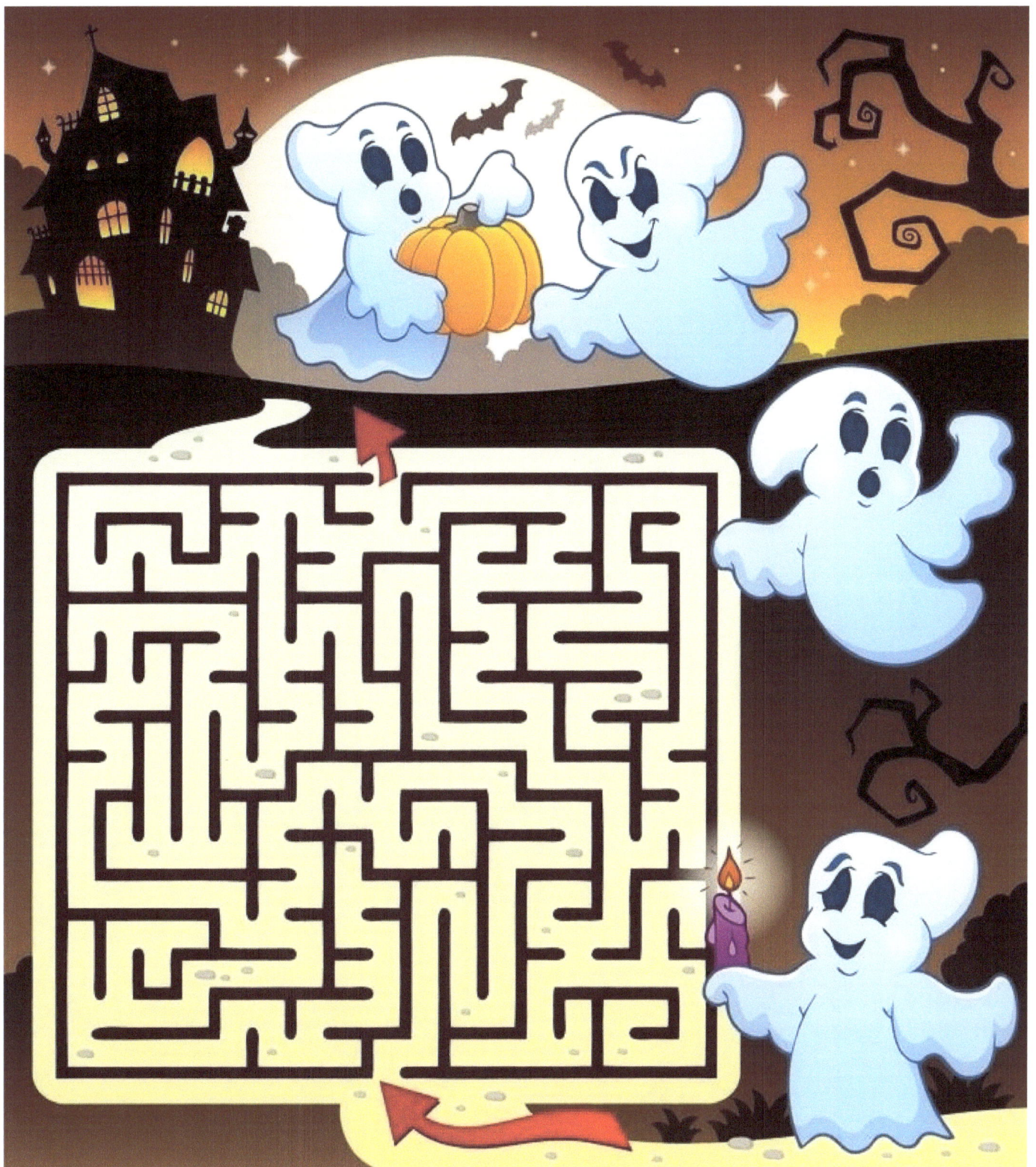

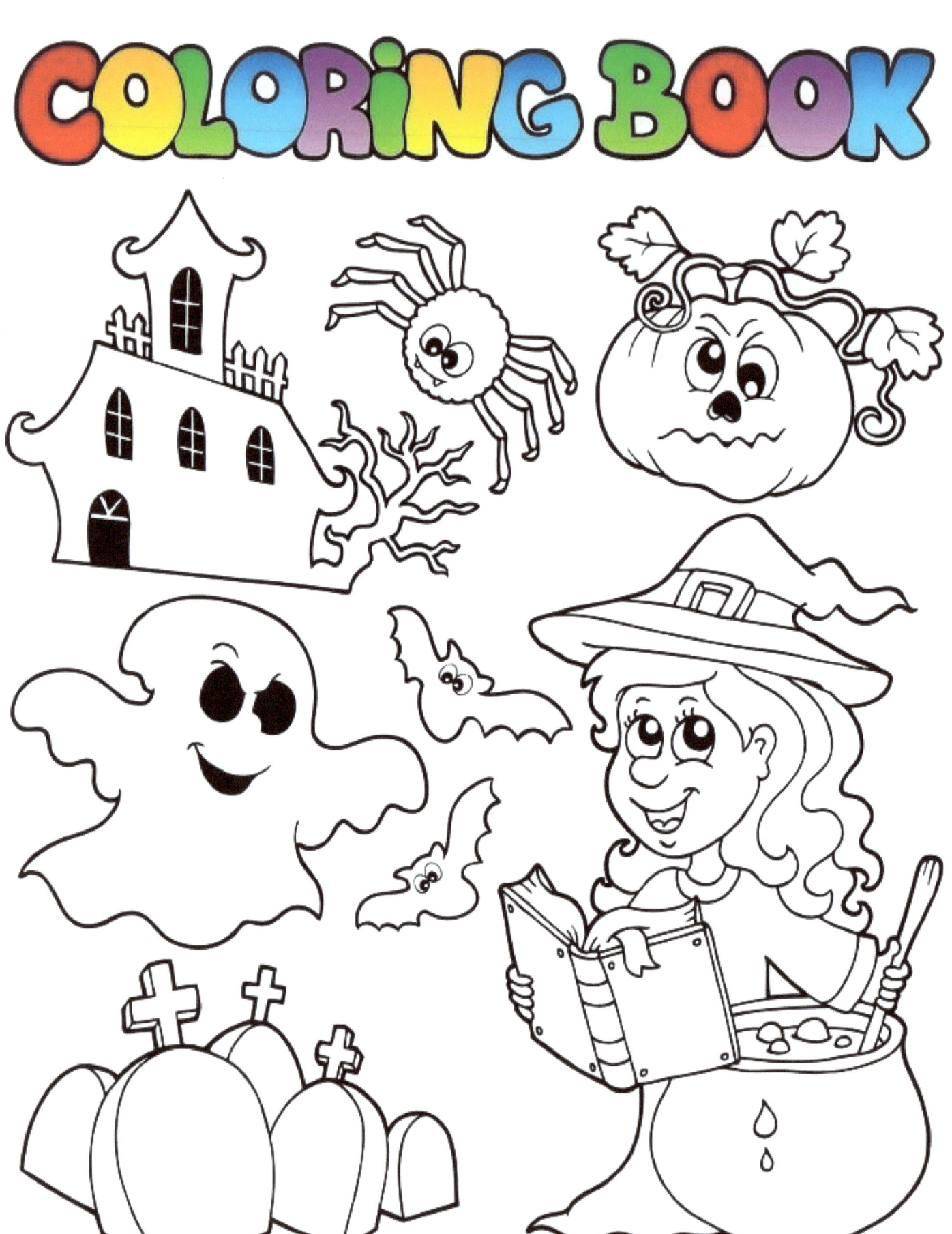

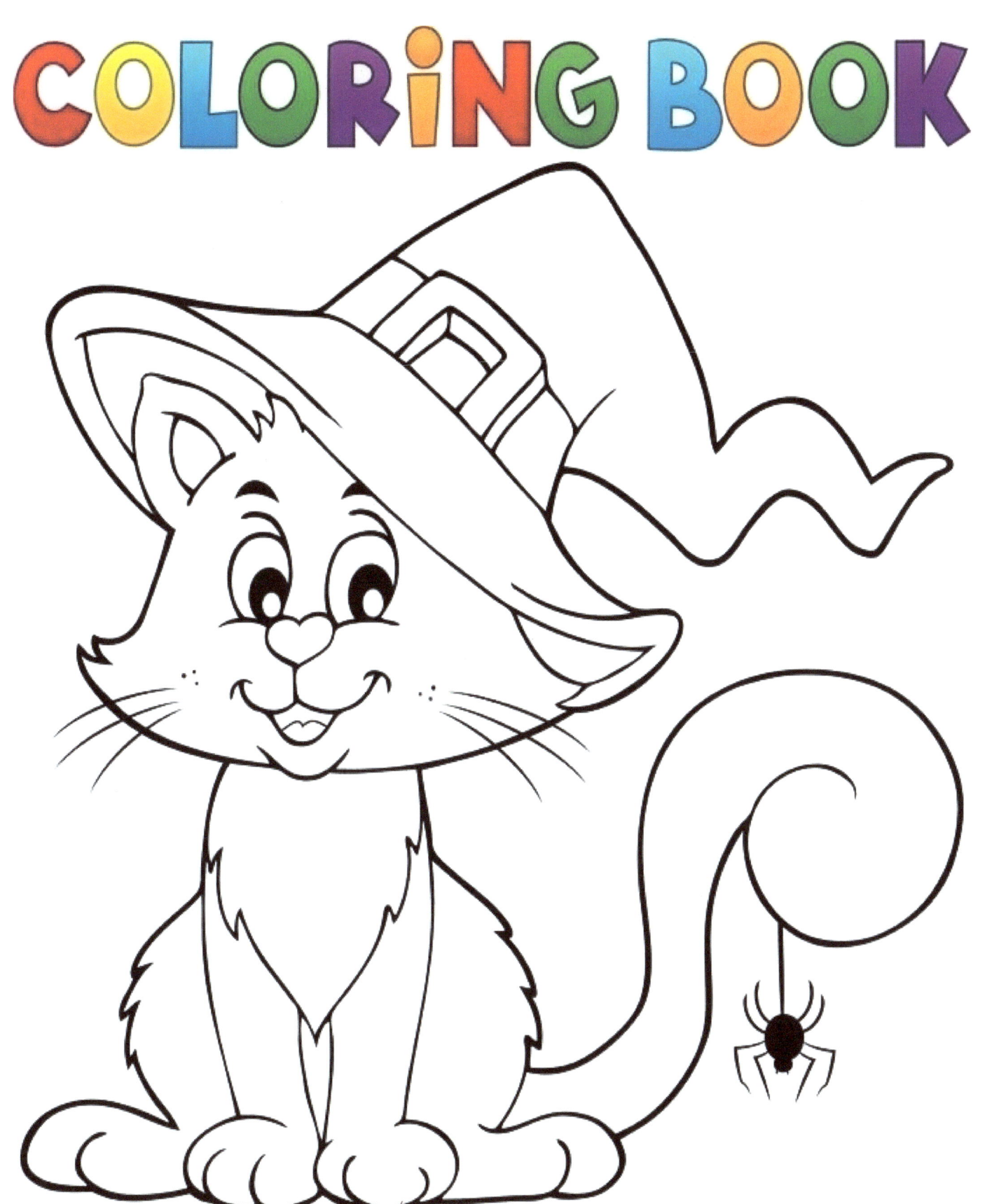

COLORING BOOK

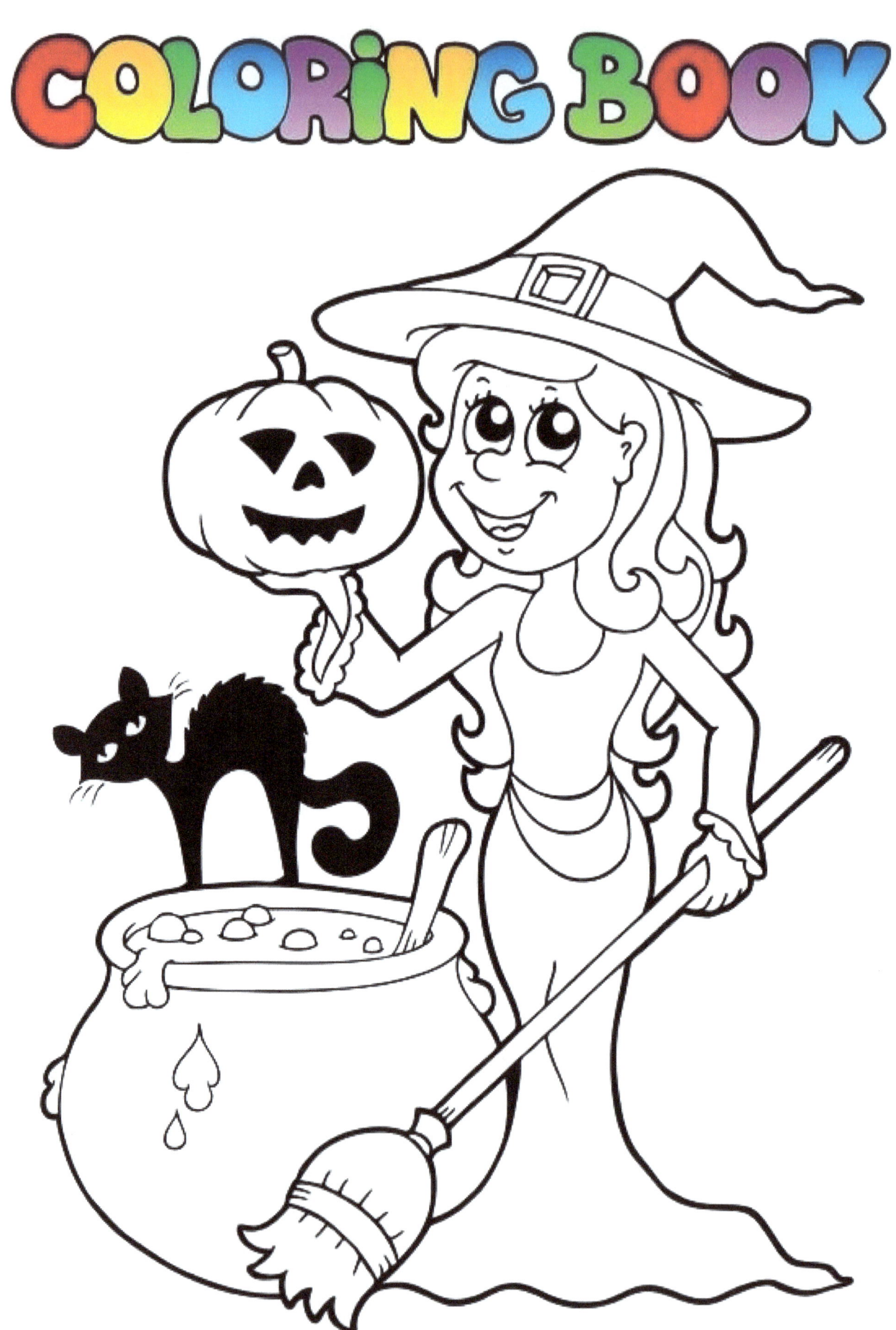

COLORING BOOK

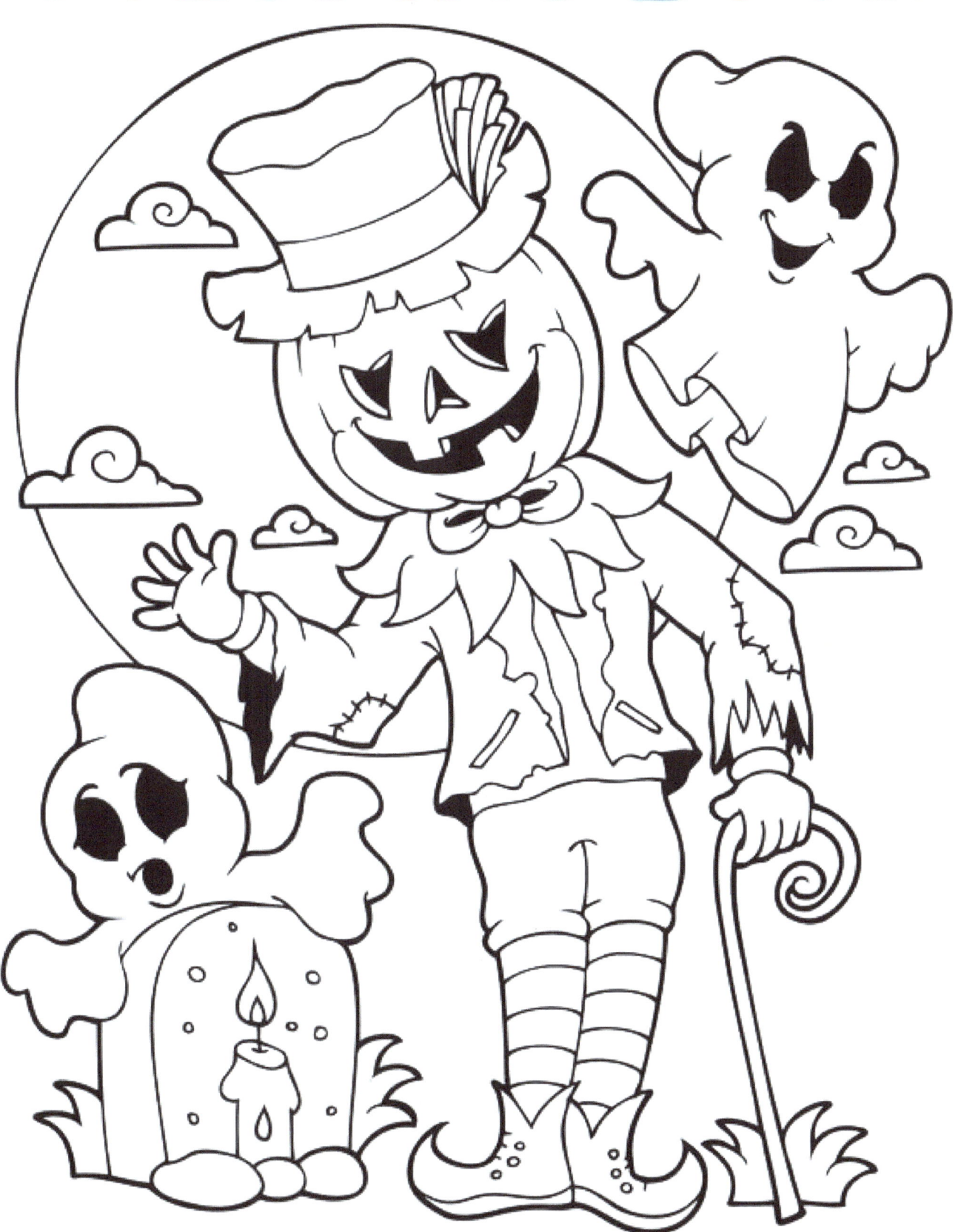

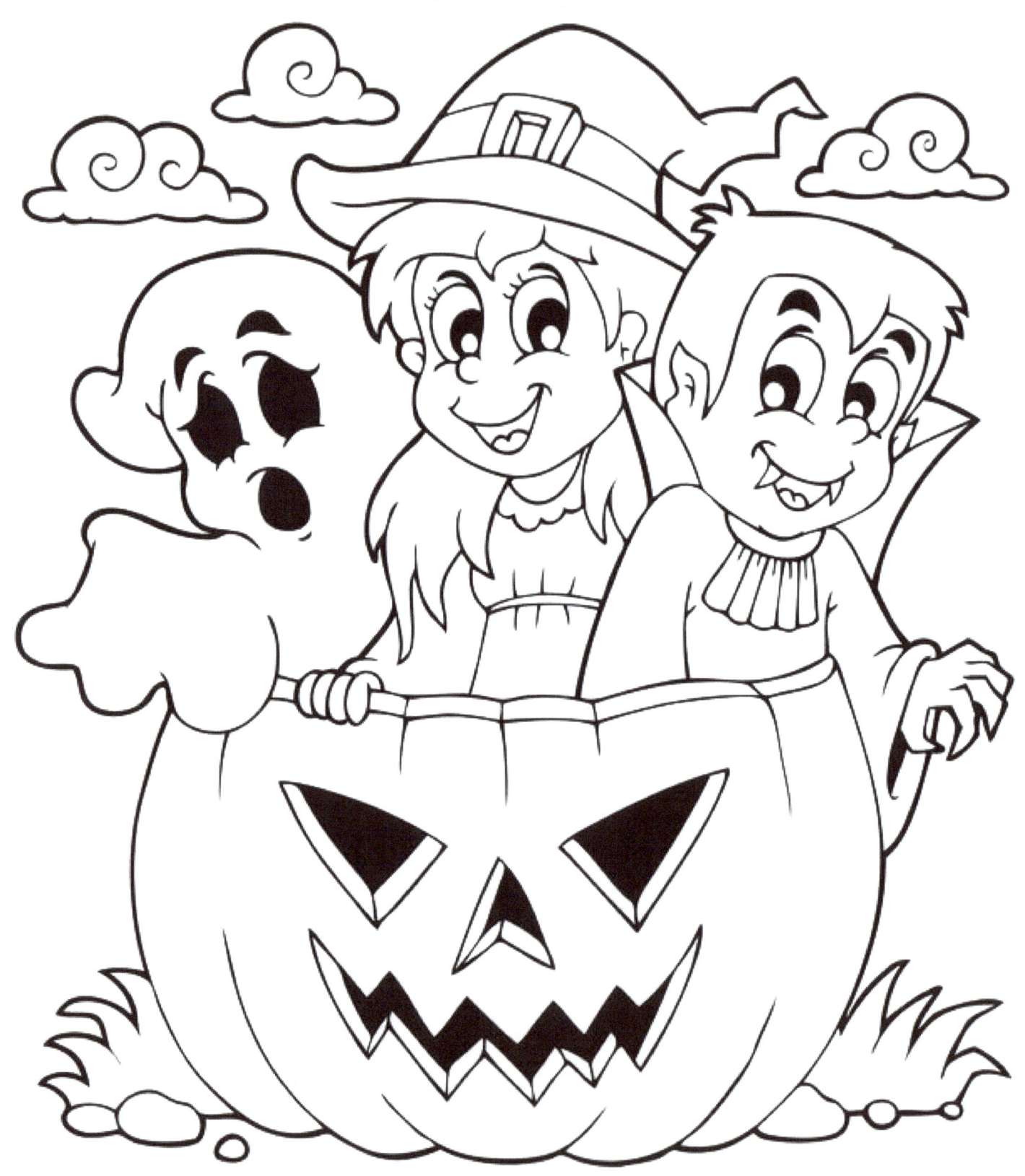

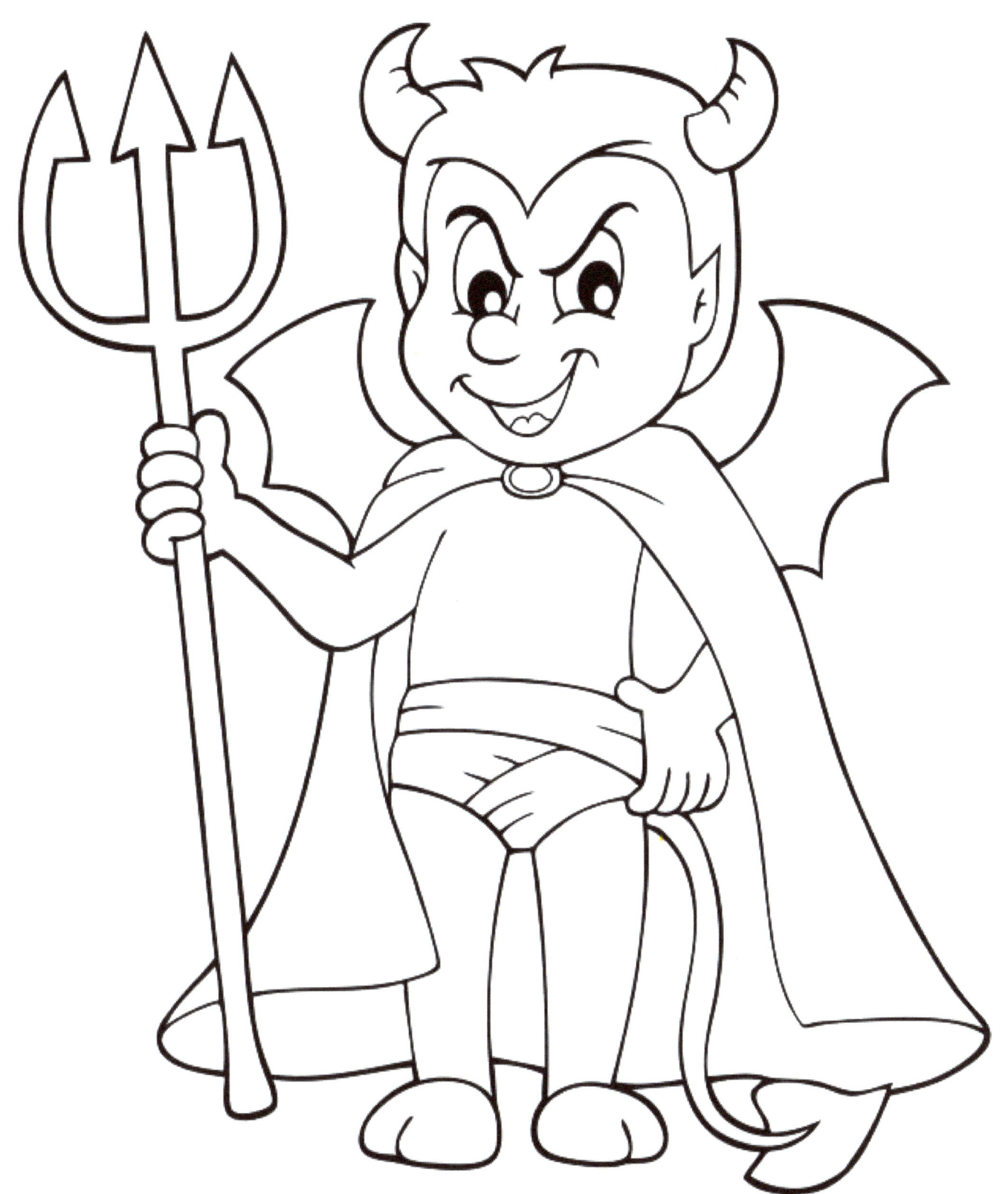

COLORING BOOK

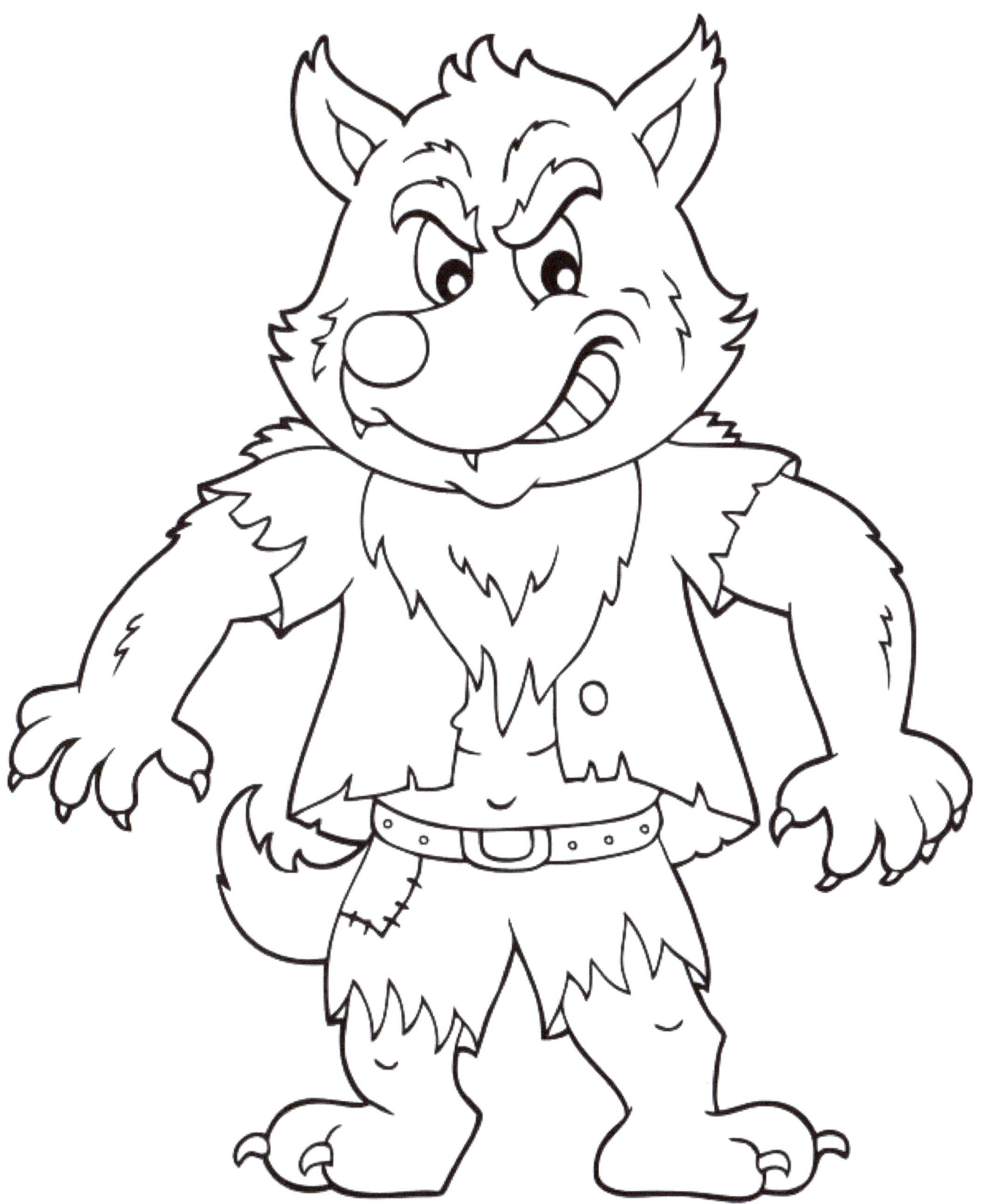

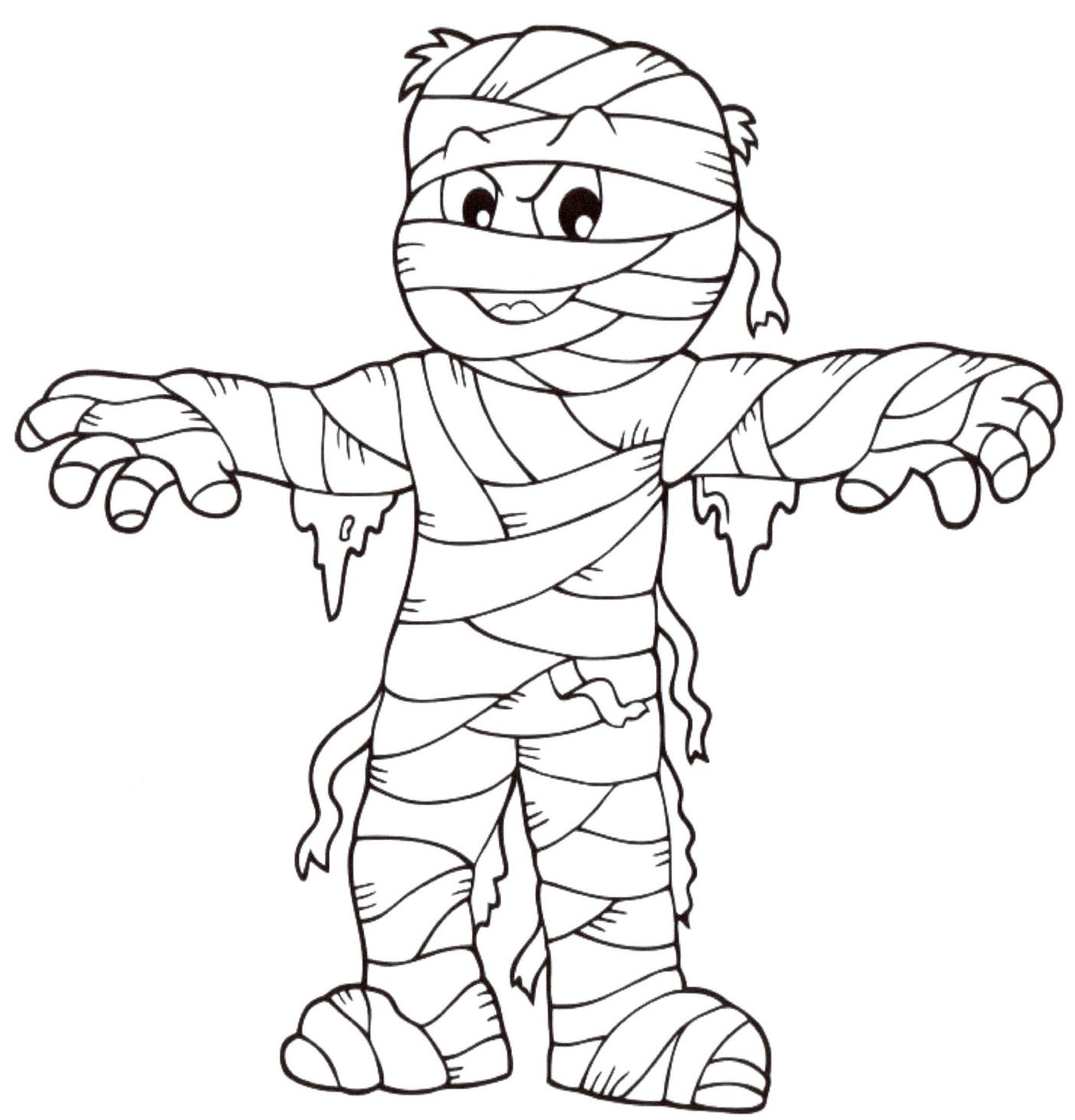

Publications Interest Form:

ambKids Academy is an advocacy project with a goal of improving state wide test scores, reading, writing, and life skills training, through learning tool workbooks, publishing books with target messages for youth in areas that will build self-esteem, healthy body image, and social-economic enrichment to better serve the youth in our communities.

Please Check all that applies:

- ☐ I am a Parent
- ☐ I am an Educator-Teacher
- ☐ I am a Professional
- ☐ I am an Author
- ☐ I am a Student

- ☐ Check here if you are interested in Publishing under ambKids

Enrichment Workbooks and Reads:

- ☐ Self-Esteem
- ☐ Healthy Eating
- ☐ Healthy Body Image
- ☐ Bullying
- ☐ Violence in Schools
- ☐ Social Skill Development
- ☐ Drug and Alcohol Abuse
- ☐ Dating

Science:

- ☐ Biology K-12
- ☐ Anatomy K-12

Math:

- ☐ Addition
- ☐ Subtraction
- ☐ Multiplication
- ☐ Division
- ☐ Fractions
- ☐ Algebra

History:

- ☐ Learning States
- ☐ Learning Continents

English:

- ☐ Spelling Sight Words
- ☐ Reading Age Appropriate

Learning Tools Workbooks:

- ☐ Matching Numbers
- ☐ Abc Flashcards
- ☐ Abc Cursive
- ☐ Colors
- ☐ Telling Time
- ☐ Matching Game
- ☐ Counting
- ☐ Educational Games

Please email us: ambkidsacademy@gmail.com

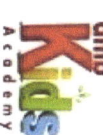